It's about time

A call to the Camino de Santiago

redemptorist
p u b l i c a t i o n s

Published by Redemptorist Publications
Wolf's Lane, Chawton, Hampshire, GU34 3HQ, UK
Tel. +44 (0)1420 88222, Fax. +44 (0)1420 88805
Email rp@rpbooks.co.uk, www.rpbooks.co.uk

A registered charity limited by guarantee
Registered in England 03261721

Copyright © Redemptorist Publications 2019
First published July 2019

Text by Johnnie Walker
Edited by Katie Stockermans
Designed by Emma Repetti
Photos by Miguel Castaño
Shutterstock.com: Foreword Image, The saint and the pilgrimage Image, Page 6 (Iryna
Savina), 7, 12, 16, 24, 29 (CZEll), 43 (alfotokunst), 49 (Natursports), 55, 57 (s_bukley), 58

ISBN 9780852315552

A CIP catalogue record for this book is available from the British Library.

The publisher gratefully acknowledges permission to use the following copyright material:
Excerpts from the *New Revised Standard Version Bible: Anglicised Edition*, copyright © 1989,
1995, Division of Christian Education of the National Council of the Churches of Christ in
the United States of America. Used by permission. All rights reserved.

Printed in Britain by Orchard Press Cheltenham Ltd.

It's about time

A call to the Camino de Santiago

Johnnie Walker

Foreword by Joyce Rupp
Conclusion by Martin Sheen

Dedication

This book is dedicated to the friends I have
made through the pilgrimage to Santiago
and to the many pilgrims who return to
serve others as volunteers.

Foreword

Fifteen years ago I hoisted my too-heavy pack onto my back, breathed a big sigh of joy mixed with a bit of apprehension, and took that first step on the path to Santiago. When I close my eyes now and pause for a moment, that initial movement seems more like yesterday than a decade and a half ago. That is how strongly this pilgrimage, with its ancient roots, implants itself in the mind and heart of those who embrace this astounding journey.

Johnnie Walker wisely writes that every pilgrim is undoubtedly changed in some way from walking the Camino de Santiago. His words certainly ring true for me. The sights and sounds of my thirty-plus days of walking the terrain in Northern Spain often return, along with images of the faces of fellow pilgrims who quickly endeared themselves to my heart. But what remains most firmly ensconced in my memory and continues to be activated in my life is the desire to live a life which is as uncluttered as possible.

The longer I journeyed on the Camino, the more I appreciated having only what I truly needed. I did not have to wonder what clothes I would wear for the day, or have lots of options to sort through in order to find something for my personal use. I discovered how little I really need to be satisfied. Everything was there on my back. And it was enough.

In this consumeristic culture that pushes to have much more than is required, being satisfied with having "just enough" can be challenging. The Camino taught me about wasting energy on worrying over what might be lost or damaged, and how much distress can be caused by being overly concerned with having every possible item with me "just in case". Immense freedom of mind and heart evolved in living simply during those weeks of walking. It also provided a sense of oneness and a compassionate

relationship with the financially impoverished people of our planet who barely have the basics required for daily existence.

Along with the central principle of living simply, the other embedded treasure from walking the Camino de Santiago has been a keen awareness that life truly is a journey. Not knowing what lies ahead, trusting the way will be made known, living each day wholeheartedly instead of fretting about tomorrow; all this developed in my consciousness and continues to guide my mind and heart towards ongoing peace.

In *It's about time*, Johnnie Walker describes this path as "a holy road." Indeed, it is. The sacred can be glimpsed everywhere: in the face of each person, in the beauty of the land, in the ups and downs and in-betweens that move within each pilgrim as he or she leans towards another layer of personal transformation. The author also provides significant details from his experience as a pilgrim that will be of excellent assistance to the person who chooses to walk the Camino. His book offers excellent advice and encouragement so I will limit suggestions of my own to the following.

Pilgrim of our beloved earth, if you choose to walk the Camino de Santiago, embrace mystery and engage in the adventure of uncertainty. Welcome without judgment other pilgrims who also walk the path. Treat citizens and residents of the country with respect. Leave the earth free of any material remnants of yours as you pass by. Receive each day with a grateful spirit. Embrace the seasonal weather without grumbling. Thank your body every day for all it does for you. Relish each step as an opportunity to draw closer to the Holy One, your trusted companion who guides your every footstep on the road to Santiago.

Buen Camino!
Joyce Rupp

Author of numerous best-selling books, including
Walk in a Relaxed Manner: Life Lessons from the Camino.

Pilgrim routes to Santiago de Compostela

Each year hundreds of thousands of people walk to Santiago de Compostela in north-west Spain. They take many routes following in the footsteps of pilgrims of the Middle Ages. The most famous route is the Camino Francés, a journey of some 800km from the border of France and Spain to Santiago de Compostela.

The saint and the pilgrimage

James was a fisherman, son of Zebedee and brother of John. Legend has it that after preaching the Gospel in Spain, James (Sant Iago) returned to Jerusalem and martyrdom. After his death it is said that James' body was transported to Spain in a stone boat. The site of his tomb in Northern Spain was lost for some 800 years until a hermit discovered the burial place. The relics were authenticated by the Church and it became a place of pilgrimage which grew into the city of Santiago de Compostela. In medieval times the pilgrimage grew in popularity and pilgrims started to flock to Santiago in huge numbers. People set off from their homes and walked from all over Europe to venerate the tomb of the apostle. Religious orders provided shelters along the way in which pilgrims could sleep, and where they cared for those who were sick or dying.

After several centuries these numbers dwindled due to a combination of war, plague and the Protestant Reformation. However, interest in the pilgrimage to Santiago never completely died and in the last fifty years there has been a great revival of enthusiasm for the Camino, the Way to Santiago.

Nowadays people of faith still walk hundreds of miles to Santiago but among the 300,000 or more who arrive on foot each year there are many others with a variety of motives. Some have lost their faith and are searching, others are spiritual people at odds with organised religion, still others walk the Camino as a bridge from one way of life to another, and others make the journey simply to enjoy the challenge.

The priest and the paintbrush

Perhaps the biggest contribution to the modern revival of the pilgrimage came from Father Elías Valiña Sampedro, the parish priest in O Cebreiro. He was a scholar who, following the historical records, marked out the many routes taken by the medieval pilgrims by painting yellow arrows at approximately every thousand paces. Therefore, pilgrims today can follow the yellow arrows from Saint Jean Pied de Port in France all the way to Santiago on the Camino Francés. Other routes include the Camino Inglés from A Coruña or Ferrol on the north coast, where the English pilgrims arrived by boat, or from Seville in the south along the Vía de la Plata. These are only a few of the many routes! The work of Fr Elías and the pilgrim associations, Los Amigos de Santiago, also helped build up a huge network of pilgrim hostels just like their medieval counterparts, and all along each route are *albergues* for rest and sleep for a donation or a small charge of a few euros.

The Pilgrim Passport and the Compostela

Everywhere pilgrims stop along the way they obtain stamps (*sellos*) on their Pilgrim Record (also called the Pilgrim Passport, or *credencial*) as evidence of their pilgrimage. This document is essential to gain admission to the pilgrim *albergues* along the way. Pilgrims who walk at least 100km to Santiago or cycle at least 200km are entitled to apply for the traditional certificate of completion, the Compostela, when they present their *credencial* at the cathedral's Pilgrims' Office.

Introduction

The bells of the cathedral have rung out over Santiago for many centuries. They chime the hours. They call the faithful to worship. With joyful peals they announce the great feasts of Easter and Christmas. And they toll mournfully to announce the Mass of the dead. The bells have witnessed many things. They hang high above the cathedral where they have watched students cavorting, pilgrims arriving in unending streams, priests and canons plotting and praying. They have rung for weddings and marked requiems. They have seen many changes… of archbishops, centuries and even a millennium.

Every day they look down on hundreds of other kinds of changes. The changes which we pilgrims resolve to make in our lives by the end of our pilgrimage. I would be surprised if there are any pilgrims who have arrived in the Plaza Obradoiro who have not in the depth of their hearts promised themselves, and perhaps others, to change in some way. I think this is at the heart of why we walk to Santiago. Contemplating change in our lives is the very stuff of pilgrimage. For me this has little to do with religion and everything to do with the spirit which motivates every pilgrim to put one foot in front of the other on the pilgrimage journey.

That journey often starts a long time before the first actual step. It is as if the peal of the bells of Santiago Cathedral reach out across countries and continents to call those who can hear them to pilgrimage. This is the story of how I, and some of my pilgrim friends, heard that call and what happened when we answered it. Perhaps you'll hear it too.

Buen Camino!
Johnnie Walker

Contents

"For everything there is a season,
and a time for every matter under heaven"

✳ Ecclesiastes 3:1

A time to dream about the Camino, and a time to try not to think about it constantly

A time to be unsure, and a time to buy the tickets

Almost twenty years ago I was invited to dinner by friends. I remember it vividly. "Come and see what Jenny has been up to," said Graham as he showed me a map of Spain on the wall. There was a red line along the top from left to right and two photographs of Jenny in walking gear which had been pinned to it at different points. Over dinner I learned that the red line was one of the routes to Santiago de Compostela, called the Camino Francés, and that Jenny had walked it in two halves at different times.

Although I had heard of the apostle Saint James, I knew little about him and whilst I'd vaguely heard of Santiago de Compostela in north-west Spain, I didn't know that Saint James was buried there or that thousands of people, like Jenny, walk there every year.

Over dinner Jenny told me about the adventure of walking almost 800km from the border of France, meeting other pilgrims from all over the world, sleeping in *albergues*, blisters, wonderful scenery, days of exhaustion and many days of joy, and the huge sense of achievement when she arrived in Santiago. That dinner conversation sparked off many hours of daydreaming and research. Could I do it… Could I?

Four years were to pass between that dinner and my departure for Spain to walk to Santiago de Compostela. During that time the idea grew, and the more I found out, the keener I became to make the pilgrimage. I've discovered that many pilgrims spend years in anticipation before the time comes when they finally make the journey.

Just before my fiftieth birthday I left a very difficult job and almost immediately took on another. However, increasingly I was mentally packing and unpacking my rucksack and spending far too much time on the internet where search engines are now accustomed to future pilgrims' keywords: lightest rucksack, warmest sleeping bag, first aid for hikers. But after that first phase of searching for answers to practical questions my mind often turned to other aspects of the pilgrimage: "Will the Camino help me to change?"

Some changes I wanted to make are easy to talk about. One of the reasons I started walking was as a bridge from one way of life to another. I wanted to give up the high-pressure jobs I had been doing in my professional career and lead a simpler way of life. I've met many pilgrims who walk for the same reason.

Other changes are more difficult to speak about openly. Whilst outwardly I appeared self-confident and successful, inside I was dissatisfied with how I had become. I found that I was questioning a lot of things in my life. I've always been involved in the Church as an organist and I have a deep interest in scripture, hymns and other religious music. But here I was, divorced with two grown-up children, each with their own issues to deal with, and I was doubting my faith and the Church more and more. Above all – if I'm honest – I was deeply uneasy that I had become driven, arrogant, over-achieving and intolerant of others. Despite all of the success and material possessions, I still felt as if I didn't have enough, wasn't appreciated enough. I knew in my heart that the roots of this lay deep in my background and childhood experiences. Working hard and playing hard were no longer sufficient antidotes. Gradually the idea of making the pilgrimage to Santiago grew as a way of taking time out to address some of these issues.

I joined the Camino association in the UK to get further information and I regularly chatted with other pilgrims on the online Camino forum. A list of these resources and the English-language pilgrim associations across the world is given at the end of this book.

Every time I thought: "This is it, I'm going to go" some anxiety would stop me. "I can't speak a lot of Spanish", "I'll never make it and have to give up halfway", "I'll get hopelessly lost". People who had already walked the Camino reassured me on all of these points and more. From others who had gone before I found out about travel, packing lists, what gear I needed... everything I needed to know.

I also bought my first guidebooks, not knowing that one day I would be writing them myself! I read everything I could about the Camino and I was particularly inspired by Joyce Rupp's book *Walk in a Relaxed Manner: Life Lessons from the Camino*. I could not have imagined that one day she would be a contributor to a book of mine. And I'd have laughed out loud if anyone had suggested that Martin Sheen would do the same.

I was running out of excuses. Work was more and more dissatisfying. A friend of mine, exactly the same age as me, dropped dead one day. It was as if I heard the bells of the Cathedral of Santiago calling out to me. It was time for the Camino to Santiago. I bought my tickets.

"Here I am, Lord.
Is it I, Lord?
I have heard you
calling in the night.
I will go, Lord..."
  ✳ Dan Schutte

Anne Born

I knew it was time to walk the Camino a full thirty-eight years before I did. What stopped me? I had convinced myself I needed lots of time, lots of money, and at least one worthy companion so I wouldn't get lost. More fears. Then I read a news article about ten years ago about a man who walked during the Holy Year with his two daughters. So I bought plane tickets for me and my son and we took off. I learned so much – some of it was understanding my motivation, but the rest was mostly practical things like what to carry and what to leave at home. And he learned just how fearless I really was. I had finally given myself the license to fail, to make the walk my own.

In the end, I found that the daily testing of my skills and my determination was what I needed all along and that the walking itself was a prayer, each step of my pilgrimage dispelling my fear. That's what keeps me going back now. I know I don't need any more than a few days to get the full benefits of walking. I know to stay in places I can afford, to share meals with fellow pilgrims to save money. My worthy companion? It's me now, all by myself when I need it, and with friends or my family at other times. I want to be that worthy companion to other pilgrims. If we get lost, we will get found together. And, odds are, if you see me on the Way, I'll be saying the prayer of the Spanish Saint Teresa of Ávila, over and over: "Nada te turbe, nada te espante."

"Let nothing disturb you,
let nothing frighten you.
All things are passing.
God never changes.
Patience obtains all things.
Whoever has God lacks nothing.
God is enough."

Saint Teresa of Ávila (1515-1582) ✳

A time to pack your rucksack, and a time to unpack it, then pack it again and again

A time to start walking, and a time to stop, exhausted

Decision taken and packing list in hand I started to assemble the gear I needed. Some pilgrims buy top-of-the-range equipment and clothes. Others pack what is in their wardrobe. What is certain is that you need good footwear and a well-fitting rucksack. I did as advised and walked an hour or so to a reputable shop so that my feet would be "walked on" and ready to try new footwear. I asked if any of the staff had done any long-distance walking. Alex, the manager appeared, asked me what I was planning to do and immediately started telling me about some of the epic trails he had walked. A characteristic of long-distance walkers is that we love to talk about it! Soon I was walking about Clapham Common in South London, where I lived, with my rucksack and boots on my practice walks. Each time I walked I put more in the rucksack as I gradually assembled the rest of the kit. A sleeping bag, lightweight towel, spare socks… I looked around for quick-drying synthetic t-shirts and underwear and I actually found that the thinnest and cheapest served best. All these years later I still have a t-shirt I wore on that first walk. Ever anxious, I even tried out my raingear at home by standing under the shower!

I had heard many people talking about the need to take the very minimum needed. "Carry no more than 10% of your body weight" is a rough rule of thumb some people use. I just ignored that. I knew best. More and more things went into the rucksack "just in case". A first aid kit sufficient for field surgery was assembled; now I take just some antiseptic and a few plasters. "It might be cold," I thought, so in went instant soup and of course for that I needed a thermos flask. "Take three sets of socks and underwear," I was told, "one to wear, one to dry after being washed, and one spare." I packed four. "What if I get lonely or can't keep up with what's happening in the world?" In went a radio to listen to the BBC World Service.

Gradually I increased the distances I was walking and on one of these walks I got a blister. It hurt. Barely was it healed when on the next practice walk it was cold and very rainy, and I was miserable. "Was this Camino thing such a good idea?" I began to wonder. The old seeds of doubt sprouted into full bloom. Then one day I met Nancy. She was a veteran of several Caminos, "years ago," she said. She was an artist and showed me some beautiful sketches she had made on one of her Caminos. "When are you leaving?" she asked, "Well, I haven't quite decided yet," I replied hesitantly. "I'm going next month," she said, "I want to spend my 83rd birthday doing some more Camino drawings before I get too old."

That was it! If she could do it, I could do it. No more excuses. I used the tickets, flew to Spain and took my first steps.

Pilgrim statues at *Monte de Gozo* – the "Hill of Joy"
Pilgrims get their first glimpse of the cathedral

On that first Camino I had decided to walk from Seville on the route called the Vía de la Plata. I discovered that all I had read about the route being well waymarked was true. I found the first arrow on the pavement outside the cathedral and then a yellow arrow on the wall opposite pointing right.

I followed the arrows and some thirty-six days and 1000 kilometres later I arrived in Santiago. Following that pilgrimage I walked the Camino Inglés from Ferrol, where the first arrow is at the port where medieval pilgrims would have arrived by ship, and then the Camino Francés from Saint Jean Pied de Port. No matter which Camino route I have walked, the yellow arrows and other signposts (called waymarks) have reliably shown me the direction.

One of the things which many pilgrims are most apprehensive about is accommodation. Nowadays there is a wide choice. On the main routes there is a well-developed network of pilgrim *albergues* offering low cost (6–10 euros) dormitory accommodation. Some operate simply on the basis of the donations pilgrims leave. Nowadays these *albergues* are generally very clean and offer hot showers and WiFi. Many also have single or twin rooms which cost a bit more. There is also a wide range of hostel and hotel accommodation for those who would like more privacy.

Often in *albergues* you'll meet other pilgrims you've seen during the day. When walking the Camino Francés, I set off on my own from Saint Jean Pied de Port, at the foot of the Pyrenees in France, on a sunny autumn day to walk the 25km across the border to Roncesvalles in Spain. Crossing the mountain pass is steep going and cannot be done in winter. This was the first Camino for most of the pilgrims walking that day and before I was halfway up the hill I'd met a number of them. First I encountered Julien, a student from France whose rucksack was even bigger than mine. He was carrying a tent and full camping gear. I said hello to a German pilgrim called Helmut who was about my age and was not looking happy at all about having to walk up such a steep hill. Two Dutch guys, who I later learned were called Daan and Bram, overtook me at one point without saying very much. I got in stride with two girls in their twenties, graduate students from the USA on exchange in Europe. We chatted when not getting puffed out by the steepness of the gradient. Near the top we met Irene from Dublin who said she was exhausted but with our company she rallied, and we four made it down to the *albergue* in the Monastery of Roncesvalles on the other side of the pass. Everyone was welcomed to a beautiful pilgrims' Mass in the monastery

chapel and we got our first Pilgrim Blessing of the journey. Daan, Bram and Julien joined us for dinner that night and there was much hilarity. We'd crossed the Pyrenees! Soon the food, wine and exhaustion of the day caught up with us and we were all in bed before lights out.

As I went to sleep in my bunk-bed I thought on the events of the first day and on the extract of a twelfth-century poem which was hanging on the wall:

"La Puerta se abre a todos. Enfermos y sanos. No solo cristianos, sin aún a paganos, a judios, herejes ociosos y vanos y más brevemente a buenos y profanes." (Poema "La Preciosa" Roncesvalles, siglo XII) "The door is open to everyone, both the sick and the healthy. Not only to Christians, but to pagans and Jews and heretics and vagabonds. To saint and to sinner."

"Well," I thought, "I'm not sure which, but I'm definitely one of those."

> "Ask, and it will be given you; search, and you will find; knock, and the door will be opened for you. For everyone who asks receives, and everyone who searches finds, and for everyone who knocks, the door will be opened."
>
> ✳ Matthew 7:7-8

3

A time to be afraid of new places and people, and a time to embrace them

A time to walk with others, and a time to walk alone

Although I had visited Spain for family holidays my ability to speak Spanish was rudimentary and I was apprehensive that I wouldn't understand local people or be able to make them understand me! I quickly learned that on the busier routes such as the Camino Francés local people are well used to pilgrims from other countries. They've been arriving for several hundred years! However, in preparation I got a phrase book and wrote out the phrases I thought I might need: "Do you have a bed?", "Do you provide food?", "Where is the Camino?" Being me, I also prepared for complete disaster but as I started to write out the contact details of everyone from the British ambassador to Spain to the local hospitals in the areas through which I would walk I was reassured to learn from other pilgrims that Spain is not a Third World country and that local tourist offices often have people who can speak English, pharmacies (called *farmacias*) have highly qualified staff who are the next best thing to a doctor, and the national emergency number 112 has operators who speak English.

However, my list of phrases was very useful in the beginning and at that time there was no phrasebook specifically for pilgrims. Don't worry though, if you are able to say, "hello", "please" and "thank you", Spaniards will appreciate your effort and help you to communicate.

Once I got started, I found that I needed this language crutch less and less. Often if I was slightly hesitant about which direction to take a local passer-by would shout and point the way. Sometimes they had enough

English to ask, "Where are you from?" "Scotland" always raised a smile and sometimes a shake of the head as if to say, "What is this crazy Scotsman doing walking through Spain?"

> "All along the way, from every stranger and fellow pilgrim, I hear the long promised blessing of 'Buen Camino'."
> ✳ Martin Sheen

As I continue to walk the Camino routes I am still struck by the respect Spanish people have for pilgrims. "*Buen Camino peregrino!*" ("Have a good Camino, pilgrim") they call from the fields or as they pass, repeating the phrase with which pilgrims greet each other on the way. You will use it, and hear it, thousands of times. Spain is still a rural country with many Spaniards working the land to eke out a living. For them, although Santiago is a distant place, they know it is the home of Saint James. In the more remote areas people still say, "Give the saint a hug for me." This is because on arrival one of the traditions for pilgrims is to mount the stairs behind the high altar and literally embrace the statue of Saint James to offer a prayer of thanksgiving for their safe arrival.

One thing I missed during those early Caminos was being able to have a proper conversation with local people since most don't speak English. I also quickly realised the danger of not knowing enough. One day I left a busy bar without paying and I was some way down the street when I remembered. I returned and tried to explain to the barman that I was embarrassed at having left without paying. I used the word "*embarazada*". Well, it sounded right. The man looked at me and laughed heartily as he took the money. I really was embarrassed later when I learned that in Spanish "*embarazada*" means "pregnant"!

My Spanish has improved a lot and I enjoy speaking with local people, but one of the greatest pleasures of the Camino is meeting and talking with pilgrims from many other countries. You will discover that there is an instant bond between pilgrims making the same journey to the same destination.

Some people you meet just for a few minutes, or walk together for a few kilometres. Some may become friends. Others you may see occasionally on the way to Santiago as your paths cross. Others you may never see again.

One day I was heading for Cáceres on the Vía de la Plata. This is a larger town which has a well-preserved, beautiful medieval centre which sits on a hill looking down on the modern town below. As I got closer I saw another pilgrim in the distance. I caught up and discovered that this was Zena, a Belgian pilgrim, who like me had set off from Seville almost 300km away. This was the first time we'd seen each other. We had much to chat about: the *albergues* we had stayed in; the magnificent Roman ruins early on; the open scenery; and the black pigs eating acorns who would eventually become the famous Spanish *jamón serrano*. "Didn't they stink?" she said and we both laughed. As the miles passed, we continued to chat and like many pilgrim conversations hers reached to the heart. "So, John, why are you doing this pilgrimage thing? Are you religious? Are you a Catholic?" I mumbled something about changing my life, my doubts about God and even bigger doubts about the Church. "What about you?" I asked as a diversionary tactic. "Oh me," she replied and with a reflective smile started to share her story. She was in her fifties and had been trapped in an abusive marriage for many years. "I had no means of getting out, we met when I was young, I knew soon after the wedding I'd made a mistake. Then the bullying started and occasionally worse. I had no job, no means of support. Where would I go? My family couldn't help. I lived a life of fear. Then one day it became so bad I realised my whole life could pass if I didn't do anything. It was time for me to change. It took some courage but I contacted a women's support organisation, left him, got temporary accommodation then a part-time job. Now I'm divorced…" and with the broadest of smiles she said, "and I'm walking to Santiago! Who would have thought I could be so happy… so free?" At that she started off ahead of me and I hung back wanting to give her the space to go at her own pace. She turned, looked me in the eye and said, "If you pray, John, please pray for me, and I'll pray for you." And she was gone. We never met again.

I knew what Zena meant. The Camino has shown me that I'm physically capable of walking long distances. But more important is the realisation that if all of my deep-rooted anxieties come to pass – if the people who love me stop loving me, if I lose all of my money, my home – then, with a few possessions packed in a rucksack, I can not only survive but be happy. This gave me a sense of freedom I had never experienced before, and which I've never lost.

It was that sense of freedom which it turned out Helmut, the German pilgrim I'd met in Roncevalles, was looking for.

Three days after our first encounter I began to walk up the steep incline to the Alto de Perdón – the "Hill of Forgiveness" which lies about 10km or so outside of Pamplona. The pilgrimage routes to Santiago are steeped in religious legends and symbols and it was here, we are told, that there once stood the chapel of Our Lady of Forgiveness (*Nuestra Señora del Perdón*).

Alto de Perdón – the "Hill of Forgiveness"

The story goes that on the climb up to the top the devil tempted a thirsty pilgrim, "I'll show you where there is a fountain with cool delicious water in exchange for your soul." The pilgrim refused and was rewarded with grace and safe passage. It was steep and I paused to rest a few times. On one of these occasions I came across Helmut. He was a big man and was almost lying by the side of the path, exhausted. I helped him to his feet and together we made our way slowly to the top to rest by the pilgrim statues and admire the vast landscape below. In the hours that followed we chatted, falteringly at first, each respecting the other's privacy. Clearly Helmut was well-to-do and he spoke about his education and business success. One achievement followed the other in what was becoming a litany of boasting. "So, what brought you here?" I asked, then immediately hoped that he didn't detect my sarcasm. He paused. Eventually he continued in a much softer voice.

"With success came a feeling of emptiness. There was no pleasure in looking at the profits any more. I started to crave excitement. Diversion. When someone gave me one line of cocaine I thought I could stop at that. But I didn't. It took grip. Not that anyone knew. One morning I looked at myself in the mirror and thought 'Helmut, it's time you did something about this.' I got down on my knees and prayed to God for the first time in years. That very day on the metro I read an article about the Camino to Santiago. That was two weeks ago and here I am. No drugs on the way to Santiago. I hope that I can make it." We chatted on and off over the next couple of days but when we reached Estella Helmut had to take a couple of days off to let his blisters heal and I kept on walking. I never saw him again but I have a feeling that he made it to Santiago and I hope he was able to make the changes he wanted to make.

As much as I enjoyed chatting and sharing with other pilgrims, I cherished some of the times when I walked on my own. I still do. I love the long open stretches of *meseta* – the vast plains of Spain where the trail seems to go endlessly to the horizon. What starts as just a walk each day sometimes becomes a time for thinking about nothing as the rhythm of step after step through beautiful landscapes induces a calm I only ever experience on the Camino. At other times that calmness becomes like a deeply reflective meditation. It is at these times I find myself thinking of the past and future and looking to the horizon, realising how little power I have to change anything but myself. When walking on my own I find myself not just wishing my fellow pilgrims well but also praying for them. At first prayer did not come easily. I had too many disagreements with the established Church. Then I remembered from years before Fr Joe Coghlan, a priest I greatly admire, saying, "If you have difficulty praying, try praying in a different way and try talking to God as you understand him, and ignore the paraphernalia. If you have problems with the Church, talk to God about them. The Church isn't God, it is simply one way to God." So, with some effort I put my doubts to one side and started to pray for others. At first it was like asking a God I wasn't sure was there to look after my children and loved ones, and the people I'd met like Zena and Helmut and the others.

> "I sought the Lord,
> and he answered me,
> and delivered me
> from all my fears."
> ✳ Psalm 34:4

✳ My call to the Camino
Matthew Lynch De Oliveira

It was my first Camino. I was inspired by my grandfather. I knew the planning and training he went through before the Camino. Upon his return, I heard his stories full of passion and respect for the Camino and the spiritual rewards it offers those who step towards Santiago. My grandfather invited me and my dad to join him on a Camino and somehow I knew it would be a milestone in my life. Perhaps I would find meaning I couldn't anticipate? Above all I thought it would be wonderful to walk the Camino Primitivo to Santiago with my grandfather and my dad.

The Camino took root in my imagination. I imagined it as a journey where each person finds out what the journey means for them. I presumed most people would have a defined purpose when they set out, and that some people would realise other purposes and meaning along the way. That intrigued me.

I read that for many the Camino cleansed and renewed their spirit. But I'd also heard complaints about litter on the trail. I had been involved in efforts in my community to clean up nearby beaches, removing trash primarily, to help keep the beaches safe and beautiful, and I found that very rewarding. So, there it all came together for me. My Camino would be a journey, a milestone, the treasure of shared memories with my grandfather and my dad, and a community service to help clean up the Camino. Once I had that idea it was indeed time for my Camino to Santiago.

"Create in me a clean heart,
O God, and put a new and
right spirit within me."
Psalm 51:10 ✳

4

A time to feel the weight of having packed too much, and a time to dump what's unnecessary

A time to feel sore, and a time to feel refreshed

My friend Nell from Dublin in Ireland tells the story of going to Mass in Triacastela on the Camino Francés: "Fr Augusto Losada Lopez encouraged us pilgrims to be kind to ourselves and to be joyous in our lives as a 'penance' for any sins. But it's Fr Augusto's final words of the Mass that are the ones that resonate: 'Remember, God doesn't count your steps or Saint James weigh your pack – what they measure is your heart, pilgrim, so look to your heart… and take care of your feet!'"

Taking care of feet is a universal topic of conversation on all of the Camino routes. Meet another pilgrim and they will usually ask where you started your Camino and then say "and how are your feet?" Many people walking long distances suffer from blisters, tendonitis and muscle strains. These are common but not inevitable. The most common cause of blisters is ill-fitting footwear and carrying too much weight. Almost every pilgrim I know packed too much in the beginning. I've already told you that when preparing for my Camino on the Vía de la Plata I had far too many things in my rucksack. Excitement and apprehension lead to us packing things "just in case". The reality is that there are shops in Spain and France and Portugal, just like everywhere else, and if you need something you can buy it. But there I was a couple of weeks into walking 1000km carrying a pack that weighed over 12kg because of my spares of everything, my thermos flask, emergency food and so on! I got a blister on the ball of my foot, then another, then one on the other foot. There are different ways of dealing with these and I won't give you the gory details here but the internet is a good source of advice for hikers and long-distance walkers. Friction, sweat and too much weight are the causes of most of the walking-related physical problems from which pilgrims suffer. I was no exception and I learned the hard way. The story of my life perhaps.

I treated the blisters and began to lighten my load. I went to the local post office to enquire about posting things home and discovered that they even provide the boxes. So I packed all of my "just in case" things: out went the thermos flask and my "survival" food supplies, the radio, the extra socks and underwear, the two extra t-shirts, 75% of the first aid kit, a paperback book I'd brought to read, a notebook in which I was going to write the story of my journey but which remained unopened, a spare belt, a compass and a Spanish phrase book. As I sealed the box and handed it over at the counter I felt the old anxiety. Would I be ok? However, the moment I lifted the lighter rucksack onto my back my worries disappeared. Over the next few days I kept the blisters scrupulously clean and covered and soon I was walking pain free. Nowadays I don't carry any more than 6.5kg, including the weight of the rucksack. That lighter pack helped with all of the aches and pains of walking day after day. Every pilgrim's feet ache by the end of a long day walking and muscles soon stiffen up once you sit down. Just look around at the end of a meal with fellow pilgrims and notice people groan as they stand; even young people walk like those several times their age. One of the greatest miracles of the Camino is that we go to bed sore and exhausted but by morning the aches and pains have disappeared and we carry on and do it all over again!

The lesson I learned was carry less, deal with the pain and start to enjoy the journey much more. A metaphor for life perhaps! It is true that in

my head and heart I carried other burdens: hurts, resentments, fears, guilt. During the long miles of the Camino most pilgrims think about these things. I would revisit situations which I wished I'd handled better, I'd pick over the bones of old arguments and hurts as if reliving them would somehow make them turn out differently. Once I was walking on the Camino Portugués which is the 615km-long route from Lisbon in

Portugal to Santiago. After Porto it is possible to walk on boardwalks along the beaches and cross over into Spain by boat. The scenery was stunning. The sun was shining and the waves were crashing onto golden sands. Walking in this beauty, I realised I had been mulling over an argument I'd had with someone five years earlier. Now, it was a serious argument which had serious consequences for me. The rights and wrongs don't matter but here I was walking along the most idyllic route imaginable while going over and over in my head, "I should have said XXX, and if they had replied YYY I should have retorted ZZZ." The reality is that I was powerless to change the past. It was gone. And the truth is other people have difficulties much greater than mine.

As that day drew to an end I caught up with two pilgrims I had seen in the distance. They were an older couple and sprightly walkers. I introduced myself. They were Jean and Amélie from Tours in France. We chatted a bit and I discovered they spoke excellent English which was a great help as I only had schoolboy French. They had started in Coimbra which lies south of Porto. We agreed that this coastal route was spectacular and the final miles slipped away as we chatted and I abandoned reopening the wounds of an old argument which had preoccupied me earlier. I was pleased when they agreed to meet for dinner because there had been few other pilgrims around that day.

Meal times on the Camino vary depending on where you are in Spain or Portugal. On the Camino Francés in Spain they are well accustomed to pilgrims needing to go to bed early and will serve dinner from 7pm in most places. In rural Spain restaurants don't open until 8.30pm or 9pm, whereas in Portugal restaurants open earlier, from around 7.30pm. There are also differences in the menus available, of course. Whilst in both countries the restaurants have à la carte menus, in Spain almost universally restaurants offer a *"menú del día"* (menu of the day). This is one of the legacies of the dictator, Franco, who legislated that restaurants should provide a reasonably priced menu for the workers of Spain. The custom is now part of Spanish life and culture. The *menú del día* usually comprises a choice of two or three starters, a second course of fish or meat and a choice of desserts. All of this, including water, bread and wine, may cost between ten and twelve euros… for everything! On some routes restaurants are now offering a *"menú del peregrino"* (a pilgrim's menu), which costs less and I find to be of lesser quality. In Portugal many places have set menus much like the menu of the day.

By the time I met up again with Jean and Amélie I was starving. We had all performed the daily pilgrim ritual on arrival: check in, get a stamp on your Pilgrim Passport, find your bed, have a shower and wash socks and underwear. We each elected to have the set menu, and as salad and soup were served we toasted each other with the local red wine. As the meal progressed we compared notes on the stages we had walked. Amélie had also suffered from blisters and we talked about how we had treated them. They laughed when I told them about all of the stuff I had decided to send home to lighten the load I was carrying. Jean asked why I had decided to walk the Camino and I explained that at first it had been a way of bridging my professional life to a new way of living. "What about you two?" I asked and as the words left my mouth I felt the atmosphere change. In the silence that followed, Amélie reached out and took her husband's hand and, his eyes glistening, he gave the slightest of nods. Amélie started the story slowly. They had a daughter whom they named Jacqueline because she had been born on 25 July, the feast of Saint James. Amélie laughed as she explained, "Jacques is the French name we give to boys, it is the equivalent of James. I've always liked the name Jacqueline and the day of her birth gave us the reason to name her after the saint." Jean sat in silence as his wife related how they had married when they were older and at first they thought they would never have children. They felt very blessed when Jacqueline came along. However, that joy turned to sadness when, at the age of eight, she was diagnosed with cancer.

Operations and treatments followed but after three years Jacqueline died just after her eleventh birthday. "So, you see," Amélie went on, "we felt we had lost everything and we wanted to do something to keep her memory alive. We kept her room the same as it had always been, her clothes still in the wardrobe." Jean cleared his throat and continued the story. "One day, coming home from the office, I noticed a yellow arrow on the pavement and then after a while another on a wall. I don't know why but I looked it up on the internet and what I saw filled me with excitement. These were the signs for the Chemin de Saint Jacques, the Way to Santiago, going right through our town. I called Amélie through and we both stared at the computer screen. We both said, almost at the same time, 'We will go on this pilgrimage to Santiago de Compostela for Jacqueline'". "But", said Amélie, "we decided to call it the "Chemin de Sainte Jacqueline." They told me about that first long pilgrimage through France and Spain, ending as all of us do in the Plaza Obradoiro. "We cried for a long time," said Amélie "but we also experienced a sense of peace we hadn't had before". "When was that?" I asked. "Oh," said Amélie, "that was eleven years ago, we have made the pilgrimage on a different route each year. One for every year of Jaqueline's life." At that their hands clasped even more tightly, "And now," said Amélie softly, "when we reach Santiago it will be time, time to stop."

At that we said goodnight and stood up to go. Stiff from walking all day then sitting for dinner, we let out a collective groan as we left the table, laughing at who groaned loudest.

The next day, refreshed, we set out early for Caminha, the last town in Portugal, where I would take the ferry across to Spain and continue on the coast and they would turn inland to join the Central Route to Santiago. I bade them farewell. Noble pilgrims who had walked for a very noble cause.

> "Come to me, all you that are weary and are carrying heavy burdens, and I will give you rest. Take my yoke upon you, and learn from me; for I am gentle and humble in heart, and you will find rest for your souls."
> ✳ Matthew 11:28-29

5

A time to feel like giving up, and a time to feel inspired by the whole experience

A time to share with others, and a time to listen

Where does Rioja wine come from? It comes from La Rioja of course, an autonomous region in Northern Spain, and the Camino Francés goes through it. There are vineyards as far as the eye can see and in season the vines are heavily laden with fat, purple grapes ready to be harvested.

Have you ever tried paella, the famous Spanish seafood and rice dish? Where does the rice come from? It comes from the vast rice fields outside of Valencia in south-east Spain. The arrows of the Camino Levante start outside the cathedral in Valencia and guide pilgrims all the way to Santiago, some 1200km almost diagonally across Spain. The route passes through some of the great cities of Spain such as Toledo, Ávila and Salamanca. On that route you walk through the "market garden" of the country, the rice fields and then the orchards which stretch to the horizon. You also pass through Castilla-La Mancha, the land of *Don Quixote,* where you will see castles on every hilltop. This is in stark contrast to the mountainous route of the Camino del Norte which runs from Irún with spectacular coastal views and beaches.

Despite all of this inspiring scenery every route is demanding in its own way. The best way of describing a journey on the Camino is a series of one-day walks from one bed to the next. Some days are harder than others, just like the rest of life. I have an entry in my diary that reads, "Today even the lone shepherd on the hill didn't wave back." He must have been having a hard day too! These are the days when the rucksack feels heavy, perhaps the weather is bad and the distance to Santiago seems to be getting longer

21

rather than shorter. We miss home comforts and familiar things. When the spirits are low finishing the journey feels impossible. These days are in the very nature of the Camino. It is what makes the journey a pilgrimage. A pilgrim keeps going through these difficult times and experience tells us that they will pass. Often quickly.

I was walking the Camino Inglés from Ferrol to Santiago with a group of friends including my friend Bridget. This 115km-long route was used by medieval pilgrims from England and Ireland and other northern European countries who travelled by sea and disembarked on the north-west coast to walk to Santiago. It takes five days to walk. The group had been eagerly anticipating their Camino but it rained heavily from the moment they got off of the plane until the moment they departed. We set off in good spirits but by day three both energy and good humour were running low. One or two of the group were grumpy. Everything was wet and it was very tiring. We were almost within sight of our lodgings when Bridget stopped in her tracks. Just stopped and stood as still as a statue. "Bridget, come on", encouraged another of the group. "I can't walk another step", she said, "I won't walk another step." Two of her friends put their arms into hers and gently lifted her forward and thus they reached the hostel. A hot shower, a large brandy and dinner with friends revived everyone. However, the next day it was raining even more heavily as we set out and the downpour continued all day. I was walking just in front of Bridget through a forest section. The rain was beating down. I heard a shout behind me. "Johnnie!" I turned. "Now I see why you do this so much," said Bridget with genuine enthusiasm, "this Camino thing is wonderful. It is like total freedom, total bliss."

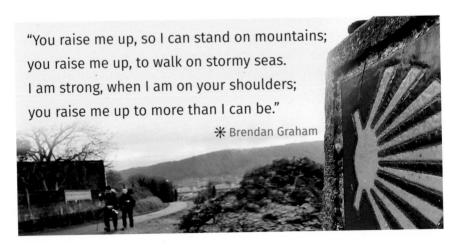

"You raise me up, so I can stand on mountains;
you raise me up, to walk on stormy seas.
I am strong, when I am on your shoulders;
you raise me up to more than I can be."

✳ Brendan Graham

One of the pieces of advice every long-distance walker needs to heed is "listen to your body". Your body tells you when you are becoming exhausted or when muscle strain or tendonitis is becoming a problem. Feeling a "hotspot" on a foot is a sign you need to stop and rest, change your socks, apply some cream or do whatever you need to do to prevent a blister from developing. If you don't and that hotspot starts to sting, that's the sign you already have a blister. It's the same with hunger and thirst. Read your guidebook for the day ahead and make sure that you have enough water, and if there are no places to stop for food carry some with you.

In addition to "listen to your body" I should add "listen to the locals", but don't suspend your own judgement! Local people will shout "*Oye*" – "Hey!" – to attract your attention if they think you are going the wrong way and point out where the arrows are. They might also try to be helpful and suggest shortcuts which work for them because of their local knowledge but don't work for pilgrims because of our reliance on following the yellow arrows. But often their advice is good.

When I came to write a guidebook to the route from Madrid, I thought I had planned well. This is not an historic route taken by medieval pilgrims but was designed by the local pilgrim association. The route runs the 320km from the Church of Santiago in the centre of Madrid to Sahagún, a town which is halfway along the Camino Francés. Designed by pilgrims for pilgrims, the trail is almost exclusively off-road on soft country paths. It is lovely. One cold day, feeling hungry, I stopped in a small town called Alcazarén, knowing it had at least one bar so I was sure I could get some food. There were no other customers as I entered and the woman behind the bar was glued to the television set on the wall. I ordered a coffee and when she wordlessly put it down in front of me I asked, "Do you have any food?" She tutted, "We don't do food." I sat sipping my coffee and feeling sorry for myself as she watched the last of her programme. It finished and as the credits were rolling on the screen she came back over to my table. "*Señor*," she said, "I've made fish soup for my family. Would you like some?" Out she came with the tureen. Delicious. "The bar may not even be open in the next village; may I make you a sandwich to take on your way?" Some advice just has to be taken.

One other piece of advice turned out to be a lesson in humility. The Camino Mozárabe is made up of the routes which start in the southern Spanish cities of Almería, Málaga and Granada and snake their way north to join the Vía de la Plata in Mérida. This is the hottest part of Spain where the houses are painted white to reflect the baking sun, and orange and lemon trees line the streets of the *pueblos blancos,* the little white painted villages which dot the hillsides. Here temperatures can reach fifty degrees in August. I enjoy the heat and I have so little hair that I always follow the advice to use lots of sun protection. The two dangers are sunburn and dehydration which can lead to sunstroke. Sensible pilgrims wear a hat.

One hot day I was walking with a friend on a long stretch of track leading to the picturesque village of Villaharta. I had been sweating a lot which made my hat uncomfortable so, having applied a good coat of factor fifty sunscreen, I was ambling along, happy and hatless. From behind us on the track an elderly man appeared out of one of the many olive groves. "*Oye,*" he shouted. We stopped and he approached. He had the deep brown leathery skin of someone who has worked in the fields all of his life. He was wearing working clothes and sporting a wide-brimmed straw hat. "How old are you?" he asked, looking me straight in the eye. I replied, "That's a strange question." He went on, "By the look of it you must be in your fifties. Old enough to know that in this sun you need to wear a hat." At that he turned to my friend and asked, "Does he not know he is completely bald?" My friend burst out laughing. I was thinking "cheeky sod". We got into conversation and he explained that his name was Segundo, which means second, because he was the second-born of the family. "I'm eighty-two and I've worked these fields all my life and I know what I'm talking about," he stated firmly. We tried to explain that modern sunscreen is really effective and I dug into my rucksack to show him the bottle. "How much is that?" he asked. Looking at the price tag he was incredulous. "Why would anyone pay for this when all you need to do is wear a hat?" He shook his head at these profligate foreigners. We had to be on our way so said farewell and I thanked him for his advice. We had only gone about 50m when I heard him shout: "*Oye, calvo, lleva su sombrero!*" ("Hey, baldy, put your hat on!"). In all humility I had to admit he was right and back on went the hat.

You will hear many other sounds on the Camino. Whether sleeping in an *albergue* or a hotel you will often be wakened by the sound of a cock crowing or a dog barking, sometimes together. In contrast, on leaving a village in the coolness of the early morning there is often nothing but a peaceful silence with no other noise than your shoes scrunching on the path and a bird singing high above. To avoid the afternoon heat some pilgrims often set off before dawn.

In Spain the morning silence is punctuated by the tooting horn of the bread van as it makes deliveries. You'll see canvas or plastic bags hanging from the front door of many houses. These are to receive the daily bread. Payment is collected at the end of the week. If you encounter the bread van as you walk they will happily sell you a freshly baked loaf.

At midday if you are anywhere near a church the Angelus bell will sound. The Angelus is the traditional Catholic prayer remembering the Incarnation of Jesus. As the bell tolls midday the prayer begins, "The Angel of the Lord declared unto Mary." Nowadays with electronic bells you will often hear the strains of the hymn being played from the belfry, "Ave, Ave, Ave Maria." There are many churches along the pilgrimage routes in Spain. Whereas in some countries churches are left open during the day, this is unusual in Spain. Generally the only time you'll find a church open in rural Spain is when there is Mass. Given the shortage of priests many small villages only have Mass occasionally. You'll know there's Mass if the church bell is rung! In larger places there may be a regular evening Mass, often with a special Pilgrim Blessing at the end.

Many pilgrims, whether believers or not, go to Mass when they can on the Camino. It is a time to reflect on the day, to pray, to meet locals and other pilgrims and to sit with weight off of tired feet. Some of these Masses are memorable. I remember one in particular. In Carrión de los Condes on the Camino Francés there is an international pilgrim Mass every evening where the nuns, who run a wonderful *albergue* in the village, sing and make everyone welcome. At the beginning Father Julio asked the pilgrims present to shout out where they were from. A glorious cacophony followed. "Italy, Australia, Ireland, America, England, France, Scotland, Latvia..." The list went on. Just when everyone thought it had stopped, a timid voice announced, "Japan" to spontaneous applause. Later in the Mass, Father Julio said in Spanish and in English, "No matter why you are on Camino or at this Mass, you are welcome. Whether you believe as we do or not, you are welcome. We pray that we are all filled with the peace of Christ." At that he invited everyone to exchange a sign of peace. The experience of a church full of pilgrims and locals embracing in peace will remain with me for a very long time. Nations united in the peace of Christ.

"Peace I leave with you; my peace I give to you. I do not give to you as the world gives. Do not let your hearts be troubled, and do not let them be afraid."

✳ John 14:27

Our call to the Camino
Matilde Rodriguez Vázquez and Xosé Lois Freire

We live in Santiago, the city in which we were both born and grew up. Our experience of the Camino was watching pilgrims in the old town, usually tall skinny people with a big backpack! They often asked for the way to the cathedral as there were no yellow arrows in the eighties. Lois' mother, Alcira, had a little hostel and during the summertime it was common to find them there. The big increase was in the Holy Year of 1993, when the regional government decided to start a huge programme to reinvigorate the Camino and its meaning.

We used to think like a lot of people here who say: "Why would I make a pilgrimage to Santiago? I already live here!" Matilde's brother Castor and his group of Scouts cycled the Camino in 1993 from France, and the family honestly thought they were mad... but brave. They had the time of their lives and it was a great adventure. The Camino is in the blood of Spanish people and before we started to go out together Lois, who is very

sporty, cycled the Camino. He dedicated his Camino to the memory of his father. When his father died, Lois just felt he had to do this. But when he spoke about it he said that walking might be better because cycling is fast and he missed spending more time with other pilgrims. One day Matilde decided it was time for her to walk to Santiago from Saint Jean Pied de Port. The story of what happened to her is told in chapter 6. The Camino changed our lives.

Together we walked the final stages to Santiago, overjoyed to reach the Plaza Obradoiro in our own city. And we celebrated our love for each other when together we walked down the aisle as we got married. We thank God for that and for the Camino de Santiago!

The Camino is infectious and as we write this, our brother-in-law, Ian from England, has walked from France and is finishing in Finisterre. The entire family is linked by the Camino.

"As for me, I would seek God,
and to God I would commit my cause.
He does great things and unsearchable,
marvellous things without number."
Job 5:8-9 ✳

6

A time to wonder at the beautiful scenery, and a time to do the laundry

A time to perform the daily routine,
and a time to be open to miracles

Walking the Camino to Santiago you will experience many things. Fellowship and solitude. You will walk through the ugly industrial approaches to some towns and you will wonder at the beauty of the mountains and valleys and the vast *meseta* (the plains) that stretch before you. But the pilgrim life isn't all gazing at scenery and taking photographs to send home. Pilgrims have a daily routine which quickly becomes established after the first few days.

If you are sleeping in *albergues* the usual routine is to have a shower on arrival and not in the morning. In the morning in most *albergues* there is time to brush your teeth, pack the last things into your rucksack, grab a quick bite of breakfast if it is provided and then set off. Most *albergues* require pilgrims to leave by 8am when the morning air is cool. In the summer months many pilgrims like to set off before dawn and there are lots of complaints about noisy early risers disturbing everyone else. If you are leaving early

please be considerate of others... and don't forget to collect anything you have left on the washing line the night before. Sometimes clothes that have been washed aren't quite dry and you'll see pilgrims with socks pinned to their rucksacks drying off as they walk along. Add some nappy pins or strong clips to your packing list for this purpose.

If breakfast isn't available in your *albergue* there is usually a bar open early even in the smallest of villages. But just in case, it is a good idea to have a reserve of nuts, dried fruits and an energy bar in your pack.

Some pilgrims sleep exclusively in *albergues* whilst on Camino. If you plan to do this you'll definitely need a sleeping bag. The level of insulation you need will depend on the time of year you are walking. Other pilgrims sleep in hostels or hotels where bedding and towels are provided. Many people find sharing a twin room in a hostel to be very economic. Nowadays many *albergues* provide single and twin room accommodation as well as beds in a dormitory.

Whilst most pilgrims carry everything they need in their rucksack, many also send their main bag ahead to the next place they are going to stay using one of the many transport services which are now available. These are advertised everywhere along the Camino routes. You can arrange to have your pack transported on the spot or in advance online. There are advantages and disadvantages of doing this. The biggest advantage is walking without the weight of all your belongings, and you only need a little day pack containing water and some food. Some people need to do this for health reasons. However, the disadvantage is that you need to prearrange where you are staying that night so that your pack can be delivered there. Some people feel that this takes the spontaneity out of their day when they prefer to stop when they are tired, or wherever their friends are stopping. There is no right or wrong in all of this. The only thing that is required is that you walk to Santiago!

The only other thing that I think is required is an openness to being surprised at what you will discover about yourself and other people. Some veteran pilgrims say, "Give yourself to the serendipity of the Camino." Others talk about "Camino angels". They are referring to the many acts of kindness which they have received from local people and other pilgrims. I was surprised by this at first. In a bar when I went to pay, my bill had been paid. Workers gathering fruit in the orchard gave me a bag of oranges. A cobbler fixed my boot and refused any payment. A country vet gave me a lift to my accommodation when I could walk no further. I have countless memories of the goodness of local people along the Camino ways. But sometimes the serendipity of the Camino is more life changing.

My friend Matilde was born and bred in Santiago. Like most people from the town she had never considered walking the Camino to Santiago... because she already lived there! Her boyfriend Lois was an exception. He's a keen athlete and had cycled the Camino Francés. I had been helping Matilde practise her English and when we met for lessons we often spoke about the Camino to Santiago. Then one day Matilde announced that she was going to walk the Camino Francés. She's a practical, no nonsense Santiago lass, who is a history teacher by profession. However, at that time, along with 25% of the Spanish population, Matilde was out of work. I suppose it was because she had time on her hands and had been listening to me and Lois droning on about the Camino that her mind turned to the possibilities of travelling to Saint Jean Pied de Port and walking back to her home. Her friends found it strange and teased her about "going all religious" and becoming a pilgrim but she had made up her mind.

We did a couple of practice walks, from Padrón to Santiago on the last stage of the Camino Portugués and from Sigüeiro on the last stage of the Camino Inglés. She seemed to me to be a natural walker with an easy rhythm and pace and I knew if she took things easy in the early stages of the Camino Francés she'd be fine.

Matilde is a woman with a strong faith and so to send her on her way we arranged a Pilgrim Blessing for her. Her family were there and it was an emotionally charged moment. They wouldn't see her for over a month. Tears flowed when her mother presented her with her scallop shell, the traditional symbol of the pilgrims to Santiago, and her father presented her walking stick. They were both duly blessed as was the pilgrim. The congregation applauded when the priest wished her the first of many "*Buen Camino*"s she would hear. Off she went. Every three or four days she sent me a brief text telling me where she was and would finish it with "no problems, no blisters". Another said, "Can't sleep in the *albergues,* I am trying to avoid the crowds." At times there was the odd typical pilgrim's photograph – we always photograph our shadows! The days went on with a few monosyllabic reports, "scenery beautiful", "weather excellent".

Something niggled in my mind that perhaps she was not entirely embracing the Camino or it was not exactly what she thought it would be. Eventually there was this text exchange: "How is everything?" "Fine." "But are you getting something out of it?" Then came the historic answer: "The Camino is a very nice walk, Johnnie, but not exactly life changing."

Truth to tell, everyone had been praying for Matilde. She was young and talented and needed a job. She needed a chance to move her life on to another place. And so I was disappointed that the Camino I had raved about so much seemed to not be displaying the force which I had felt on my first pilgrimage. A few days passed. "Matilde must be within reach of Santiago" I thought. Then I got a message: "Johnnie can you contact me urgently, there has been a miracle."

Two years previously Matilde had submitted her CV as a teacher to the local authority in Sarria. She heard nothing from them. That very day as she followed the Camino through the woods at Sarria, her phone rang. It was the Director of Education. They needed a teacher immediately. "Could you start teaching at a school in Sarria tomorrow?" She did, and reported to the school twenty hours after she left the Camino. As she looked out of the classroom she was astonished to see pilgrims walking past. The school is on the Camino. She had to quickly find an apartment as commuting from Santiago, over 100km away, was not an option. She found one which was ideal. It was right on the Camino and every morning Matilde followed the yellow arrows to school. That job led to another, then her selection as a permanent teacher.

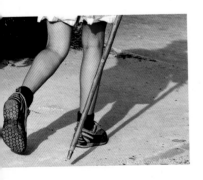

"The Camino is not a life-changing experience" – she'll never live that down! It was a very grateful Matilde who eventually married Lois and together they finished her pilgrimage, collected her Compostela and hugged Saint James. She says that she was blessed before she started her Camino, blessed in Sarria when she got the job and then blessed in the Cathedral of Santiago at the end of her journey.

Santiago Pilgrim Blessing

– used at the end of the pilgrims' Mass

Loving God, we ask your blessing on these pilgrims who have come to venerate the tomb of your apostle Santiago. As you kept them safe on their Camino way, may you keep them safe on their journey home. And, inspired by their experience here, may they live out the values of the Gospel as their pilgrimage through life continues. We ask Saint James to intercede for us as we ask this in the name of Jesus Christ, your Son and our Redeemer. Amen.

7

A time to be with others, and a time to be on your own

A time to accept the gifts of the Camino,
and a time to learn what giving means

Sometimes people say to me, "I'm going on the pilgrimage on my own. Will I meet others? Will I make friends?" These days some address this anxiety through social media and try to find others who may be starting out at the same time. The reality is that nowadays over 300,000 pilgrims walk into Santiago each year and there are hundreds of thousands more who walk part of a Camino route hoping to return in future to finish it. Many Spanish people walk a section of a route at weekends or when they have days off from work. Depending on the time of the year, many routes can be busy! When I set off from Saint Jean Pied de Port to walk the Camino Francés in the autumn I met other pilgrims with whom I would walk for many days ahead. When I set off from Seville on 2 January, albeit some years ago, I never met another pilgrim for twenty-one days until I reached Salamanca, which is about halfway to Santiago.

I discovered that I often enjoy walking on my own for long periods but that I also enjoy the companionship of others from time to time. Pilgrims talk about their "Camino families", friends they make along the way who form a group. For some of the time they may walk together or separately when someone wants to be alone. Usually they meet up in the evenings for a shared meal in an *albergue* or a restaurant.

Whilst pilgrimage is a time set apart from normal life to make a journey to a holy place, in many ways it isn't all that different from our regular daily lives. I've met people I liked instantly and others I didn't. I've met pilgrims who irritated me because they wouldn't stop talking or asked too many questions. I've had friends who had things stolen in their *albergue* or in a restaurant. Just like normal life we have to exercise our own judgement. If you don't want to walk with someone, just walk faster or slower or linger in the hotel or restaurant whilst they go ahead. As for personal safety, the Camino is a very safe place with little crime but that doesn't mean we should forget the usual precautions we would take anywhere else.

I've made good friends whilst walking the Camino and we remain in touch many years later. My best friend Stephen and I go walking together frequently and that friendship has endured and deepened through our pilgrimage experiences. These friendships are the greatest gifts of the Camino.

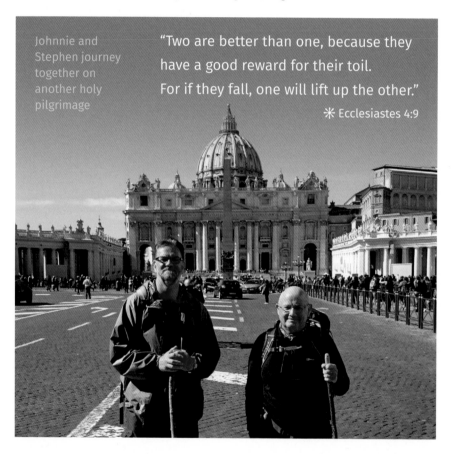

Johnnie and Stephen journey together on another holy pilgrimage

"Two are better than one, because they have a good reward for their toil. For if they fall, one will lift up the other."

✳ Ecclesiastes 4:9

One day one of these friends, Joos Bol from Holland, told me about his experiences on the "88 Temple" pilgrimage route on the Japanese island of Shikoku, which is the smallest island of Japan. Around the circumference of the island are eighty-eight temples associated with the eighth-century Buddhist monk Kōbō Daish. I decided to experience it myself.

Gifts for passing pilgrims on Shikoku

I had been taught about the phrase in the Bible "it is better to give than receive" but it would be this pilgrimage which would teach me more about giving than any other.

Some 1200km long, it is demanding at every level. The temples, the scenery, the food, the culture, other pilgrims, all coalesce to make the experience special. But there is a unique feature to the "88 Temple" route which sets it apart and made it an extraordinary experience for me. I had read about the practice of *osettai* before I left. *Osettai* are gifts which locals give to passing walking pilgrims. I had read to expect locals to offer me drinks or fruit, some nuts or even a sandwich. There are one or two websites where the authors give a daily account along the lines of, "Walked 23km, paid 30€ for bed and breakfast, received three *osettai* today – green tea, a biscuit and two mandarin oranges." Before I arrived, I thought that this was a quaint custom like the few places on the Camino routes where locals leave out fruit for pilgrims. Little did I know.

In Japanese culture politeness has been elevated to an art form. My friend Stephen and I went together and we were immediately struck by how helpful and polite Japanese people are, to the point where it appeared to border on servility to our Western eyes. I came to understand the difference between ritual politeness typified by bowing – everyone bows and the deeper the bow you give, the deeper the bow you will get back. On the train the ticket checker bows to everyone even when leaving the carriage. This act of respect is symbolic of how helpful Japanese people are, often to an extraordinary degree. During our pilgrimage everyone we asked for directions or assistance went out of their way to help. Not just once, every time. A typical example was asking a man in a garage for directions. He pointed the way. We had walked on for about five minutes when he drove up in his car. He had closed the garage and followed us to make sure we had not got lost. Another time we arrived in a town starving. Little was open and we came upon a place selling pizzas but they had run out of dough. We sat at one of the tables having a drink to make a plan for where we might eat before we found our accommodation. Around fifteen minutes later a pizza appeared in front of us. One of the customers eating at a nearby table had seen our plight, got in his car, driven to a nearby pizza shop, purchased a pizza and delivered it to us. We tried to give him money and he was almost offended. These are just a few of the many, many examples of kindness we received from Japanese people. Then the *osettai* started.

On the first day a woman appeared at the front gate of her cottage. "*Osettai*" she declared and held out a tray carrying ice-cold tins of green tea and biscuits. From that moment every day was like being showered with kindness. The *osettai* we received are too numerous to list. Strangers in a supermarket would put cakes or sweets in our bags after we had paid, bills were paid for us in restaurants, walking along the road a car would stop and hand us a bag of fruit, or chocolate. People came out of their homes with artefacts they had made or home-made delicacies. On a bus one day another pilgrim went forward and paid our fare without saying a word. The other passengers applauded us when we got off. A priest in a church we visited gave us an envelope containing the equivalent of 100 euros. A woman had handed it in: dinners for the pilgrims.

We met a Western pilgrim who eventually gave up and went home who thought this was all a little patronising. He said he felt like he was being patted on the head. I never once felt like that. I did wonder how much of this gift-giving was superstition; be kind to a pilgrim and get good luck. There may be an element of that. However, the thing that struck me most was the look of pleasure on the face of every single person who gave us *osettai*. The Biblical lesson "it is better to give than receive" is being lived on Shikoku on a grand scale.

Over the fifty days of walking the gifts did not stop. They came in the most surprising forms and often when we least expected it. While we were walking alongside a busy road, a car stopped and halted the long line of traffic. The window rolled down and a hand emerged with a box of chocolates. Another day a woman emerged from her roadside home and pressed coins into our hands. "Stop for coffee" she said in broken English. On another road a car stopped. "Are you pilgrims walking all the way today?" enquired the young Japanese man. When we said "yes" he reappeared with two packed lunches. "You must eat, pilgrims" he said, and drove off with a wave.

At the start I was a bit embarrassed about taking these gifts. I felt guilty. I can afford to buy everything I need and the gifts came from ordinary working people. I also felt a little like a spectacle. Pilgrims singled out. But as the days wore on I began to realise that I needed to accept these gifts with better grace. They were acts of generosity by people who simply wanted to give without question or qualification. That bothered me more and more because of the growing realisation that although I think of myself as a generous person, thinking nothing of buying lunch or gifts for friends, actually my giving has been very judgmental. Lunch for friends but not a penny to the beggar in the street, "Let them work as I had to" being amongst my more charitable thoughts. And yet here were these Japanese people giving to a stranger, a foreigner, unconditionally.

We struggled up the mountain to Temple 66 through rain, hail, sleet and snow. Everything was wet. The wind was an icy blast chilling us to the bone. We reached the temple and sought shelter to change into dry clothes before making our descent. The day was bitterly cold and when we reached the road at the bottom of the hill we wondered where we might get some hot food. We were gathering our thoughts and feeling very sorry for ourselves when a very elderly man on an ancient bicycle approached. Looking as if he was in his late eighties or nineties he moved the pedals laboriously until he came to a stop beside us. From a broken plastic crate attached with string he handed us two parcels wrapped in newspaper. They radiated heat. He had roasted potatoes on the fire at home on this coldest of days. Hot food for the pilgrims.

That one act of kindness from that old man was a moment of realisation. I saw that the islanders and their *osettai* were a powerful demonstration that people are capable of great goodness. The *osettai* were for me the affirmation that in this world individual acts of kindness which might seem small can count for a huge amount. My role is not to change everything around me. What I have to do is to become less mean and judgmental and place fewer conditions on what I give emotionally and materially. I have to become the change that I want to see in others and the world.

What were the gifts of this pilgrimage? A roast potato and a whole lot more.

"In all this I have given you an example that by such work we must support the weak, remembering the words of the Lord Jesus, for he himself said, 'It is more blessed to give than to receive.'"

✳ Acts 20:35

My call to the Camino

Darren Combrink

It all started one day when I was driving to work. I asked myself, "Why am I doing this?" I worked for a large corporate company in Human Resources IT. Sadly, office hours were spent at my desk, comfort eating with little to no exercise.

A good friend of mine had spoken to me about the Camino de Santiago. I did not think a couch potato could ever walk 800km across Northern Spain, or any other country for that matter. The thought of a hostel and a shared bathroom blew my mind... and not in a good way.

However, when the company offered voluntary severance packages, I signed on the dotted line and shortly after that I started the Camino de Santiago in Saint Jean Pied de Port, not knowing what was in store for me. The word "nervous" doesn't begin to describe how I felt that first day.

I had many amazing experiences on the Camino. Some really stand out. I set off from Foncebadón at 7.30am and met Neil from Ireland. We started chatting about our lives. Neil owned a couple of travel agencies in Ireland

and retired at the age of forty-two. What an amazing person to meet. When I told him what I had in mind for a future career he passed on some valuable advice. He told me to never let your need for money ruin your passion and always try to keep a balance in life. At that moment I had a view of the Cruz de Ferro, the clouds moved away, the sun came out and the view was spectacular. It was a very emotional time for me on that mountain. I just knew my next life instalment would be in the travel industry. When I got home I studied to become a tour guide and started my own company.

I've now walked six Caminos and I realised that I need to put something back. I became involved in the pilgrim association in South Africa and I've volunteered at the Pilgrim Office in Santiago de Compostela.

But it was time for me to do more and so I launched #WalkingForLife and walked the Camino Del Norte to raise funds for kids with leukaemia in South Africa. One of the best experiences of all was walking the route to Finisterre and Muxía with my partner Robert. Did the Camino change my life? You could say so!

"Happy are those who find wisdom,
and those who get understanding,
for her income is better than silver,
and her revenue better than gold."
Proverbs 3:13-14 ✳

8

A time to hurt,
and a time to heal

A time to find out what matters,
and a time to decide what doesn't matter

"This is not a walk in the park" gasped my friend Rosemary as she huffed and puffed up a hill on the Camino Inglés. It is a lovely route and on three of the days pilgrims have some cardiovascular exercise to do going uphill for about the first hour. The scenery is worth the effort. Rosemary is a fit golfer and coped well but I know exactly what she meant. Whilst the Camino could be approached as simply a series of day walks strung together in one long journey, without some preparation and exercise it can lead to blisters and muscle strain. The vast majority of pilgrims get no more than the odd blister, or aches and pains which can be dealt with by resting. Literally putting your feet up at the end of the day and, in the case of muscle strain or tendonitis, applying a cooling icepack should do it. If anything more serious develops, there are health facilities on all of the main Camino routes. In Spain, Portugal and France the health services are excellent but make sure you have adequate health insurance.

To be honest in all of the thousands of kilometres I've walked, the worst that's happened to me is getting blisters, especially in those early days. But they hurt at the time and I found that wearing slightly bigger shoes and putting some adhesive tape over the vulnerable areas solved the problem. And just like Rosemary and every other pilgrim, I know too well that dull ache in our feet at the end of a long day walking which soon goes away after a rest, a shower and a cold beer.

There are other hurts though which can't be dealt with quite so easily. Pilgrimage for me is a time when I can face what has really hurt in my life and I've discovered that the walking, step after step, becomes like a balm for my troubled heart. It is on pilgrimage that, without even trying, my mind turns to the things that have gone wrong in my life: the hurt look in my parents' faces when I didn't choose the career they thought I should have chosen or marry "the right kind of girl" according to their definition; my hurt at their disapproving silence when I told them that after twenty years of marriage we were separating; the childhood incidents which in an instant I could relive; and of course the realisation that although I've always liked to think of myself as the person who was hurt, I have also inflicted hurts on others. I was also aware of my jealousy of people of faith. The people I saw in church praying earnestly. I'd tried that and felt it didn't work for me. I'd looked for signs that the God they spoke about existed. I tried very hard but I thought nothing came. Until I discovered the Camino to Santiago.

There, slowly in the heat of the long *meseta*, I saw the world was a lot bigger than me. In the mountains I saw the raw power of a waterfall, the stately form of a startled deer, an exquisite wild flower blossoming. Across my path I watched the ants and caterpillars march with some purpose of their own. Above, the eagles circled high. Heat and distance and solitude. Sweat on my back and a dull ache in my toes. Mile after mile, never a thought of stopping, of just chucking it. Calling a taxi never entered my head. Not once. For all of its pain, the Camino was too good.

It became a series of experiences I find difficult to describe. The way my heart skipped a beat to catch a glimpse of a figure on the horizon. Another pilgrim! Walking faster to catch up with them, the excitement of meeting another human being – someone else in the lifeboat. The pleasure I felt when looking up at a sun-drenched hill on a long afternoon to see a shepherd lift his arm in greeting. The conversations I had with a dog that followed me for miles. Could I ever admit to this? Swapping recipes with an elderly lady in a bar. The old man with the bad knees who almost died laughing when invited to come along and hug the saint himself. The spunky nun all in black in Valencia Cathedral who gave me the first *sello* and responded to my invitation to come walking with me to Santiago with, "When do we leave?" The other nuns shrieked with laughter.

Enjoying the profound silence of the morning. Often precious moments of deep reflection. Often not thinking about anything. Brainwashing in the best sense. Enjoying walking alone and then coming together with my *compañero* to chart the way forward. Talking about the world, politics, singing old songs and inventing new ones, discussing what those ants who are marching across the trail in double columns might be planning.

Could a cold beer taste more delicious than the first glass on arrival? It's one of those special moments only pilgrims know about. When the pack is laid down and you feel the throbbing of relief when you sit and the weight comes off weary feet, boots off and toes curling in delight at the freedom. The heaven of a long hot shower is trumped only by the bliss on those evenings when a hot bath is available. Reviewing the day over dinner and planning tomorrow over dessert.

And in the midst of all of this I pray. I don't know when my conversations with God began but little by little I started to tell this God, whose existence I was still unsure of, about everything: my fears; my guilt; my reasons; my excuses; my worries. And my growing feeling of being glad to be alive. As I walked I felt there were things I should now let go of. I began to accept that the people who had hurt me had themselves been hurt too. I came to admit that there were certain things in my life which were in the past and could not be

> "We cannot measure how You heal
> or answer every sufferer's prayer,
> yet we believe Your grace responds
> where faith and doubt unite to care."
> ✳ David Ball, John L Bell, Graham Maule

undone, no matter how much I ruminated about them. All I can tell you is that I'm still walking and I'm still praying and mostly in my life I have a sense of peace that I didn't have before. There was no blinding moment of conversion, no magic formula, just walking the Camino.

Some people say that the Camino only works if you do it the "correct way". In any group of pilgrims this will be a hot topic. Some will argue that you aren't a real pilgrim if you don't sleep in *albergues* and carry everything you need in your rucksack. Others say a pilgrimage is only a pilgrimage because of prayer, and if you don't pray, it is simply a hike. "No pain, no gain" is a particularly grim slogan regarding blisters and sore muscles by those who believe that the Camino has to hurt to be effective.

My own view is simple. Take time out to make the pilgrimage by walking a Camino route to Santiago and let the journey do the rest. When I hear pilgrims arguing about this I say, "It doesn't matter."

It doesn't matter whether you walk a route where you won't meet anyone else, or walk the Camino Francés and meet thousands of others.

It doesn't matter whether you sleep in hotels and hostels during your journey, or share accommodation with other pilgrims in *albergues*.

It doesn't matter whether you take every detour to the holy places traditionally visited by the medieval pilgrims, or walk straight to Santiago in the shortest time possible.

If doesn't matter whether you carry every item of kit on your back each day, or arrange to have your luggage carried forward to your next destination.

It doesn't matter whether you eat from the à la carte menu in restaurants and enjoy good wine, or eat the *menú del día* for 8€.

It doesn't matter whether you give according to your means in *albergues* and churches, or give a minimum donation.

It doesn't matter whether you journey in reflective silence, eschewing modern technology, or take your iPod, iPhone, netbook and other gadgets.

It doesn't matter whether you buy designer walking clothes and top-of-the-range kit, or spend the minimum equipping yourself.

It doesn't matter whether you train for months, walking every day with a full rucksack, or just pack your bags and go.

It doesn't matter whether you get blisters, tendonitis and muscle strain, or enjoy a pain-free pilgrimage.

It doesn't matter whether you pray every day, visit every church and go to Mass every evening, or wouldn't step foot in a church.

The **only** thing that matters is that wherever you start, you walk each step of the way to Santiago and treat it and its traditions with respect. It is a holy road.

Within a few minutes of meeting Pepe one day on the Camino Portugués Central Route he gave me a lecture about what makes a real pilgrim. This route is the historic way which pilgrims from the south of Portugal walked in the Middle Ages, travelling from Lisbon north to Porto and then onward to Spain and Santiago. The route from Lisbon to Santiago is 615km long, and from Porto 240km. Pepe had started some distance south of Porto, where I had started, and was already an expert. He was actually a very nice and interesting man but he was very judgmental. "Look at those '*turigrinos*'!" he would say disparagingly, pointing at pilgrims carrying only little day packs. "I bet these 'tourists pretending to be pilgrims (*turigrinos*)' have had their bags forwarded to a four-star hotel where they'll have a long bath and a slap-up meal." I didn't tell Pepe that, although I was carrying my own rucksack, that was exactly what I planned for the evening. Pepe was also a know-all. A real Camino expert. After he had corrected me several times when we were discussing different aspects of the route I decided just to keep my mouth shut. When we reached Barcelos we bade each other farewell and I thought I'd never see him again.

Over a year later I was walking the beautiful route from Santiago to Finisterre and Muxía. The name Finisterre literally translates as "end of the world" and, like many other promontories, it was thought to be so until Christopher Columbus discovered otherwise. It was also the final destination of many of the pilgrims who made the journey to Santiago in past centuries. There are various explanations as to how this continuation came about (one is that it was based on a pre-Christian route to the pagan temple of Ara Solis in Finisterre, erected to honour the sun) but is it also known that a pilgrim infrastructure existed en route to Finisterre, with pilgrim hospitals in the towns and villages of Cée, Corcubión, Finisterre and elsewhere. Pilgrims in past centuries also continued northwards up the coast to the Santuario de Nuestra Señora de la Barca in Muxía, 29km north where, it is said, the Virgin Mary arrived in a stone boat to encourage Saint James in his work of converting people to Christianity.

Near the village of Linares I bumped into Pepe again. He was walking with his wife. "This is Maria's first Camino so I thought I'd start her off with a gentle route," said Pepe pompously. There are two ways of walking this route, either by going straight to Finisterre and then around the coast to Muxía or, as I had done, walking to Muxía first then on to Finisterre. Although there is a bridge now, at that time the river at Linares had to be crossed via stepping stones where you had to take off your boots and socks. I had made that crossing about an hour before I met Pepe and Maria. There had been recent rain and the river was higher than normal. I said to them, "I found the stepping stones slippery, the water was over my ankles and to avoid losing my balance I put my boots in my rucksack and used a stick for balance." "I never use a stick", retorted Pepe, "and I know that crossing well. We'll be fine." With that we wished each other "*Buen Camino*" and went our separate ways.

A few days later I went to the pilgrims' Mass at noon in the cathedral in Santiago. It was packed with a thousand pilgrims and visitors all waiting for the Mass to begin. I squeezed into a pew and was amazed to see Pepe and Maria sitting right in front of me. I tapped Maria on the shoulder and offered her my congratulations on finishing her Camino. "How did you get on with the stepping stones?" I asked. Pepe looked shamefaced and Maria burst out laughing. "I put my boots in my pack and used a stick for balance," she replied, "but the pilgrim," she said, digging her husband in the ribs, "the pilgrim fell in."

"Pride goes before destruction, and a haughty spirit before a fall."

✳ Proverbs 16:18

A time to arrive and give thanks

A time to plan the next Camino

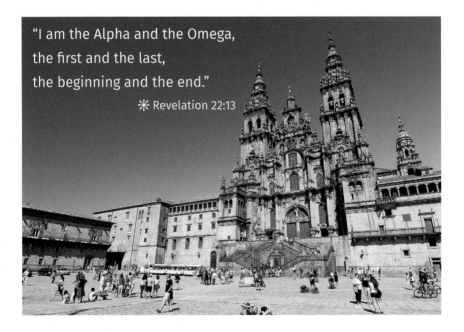

"I am the Alpha and the Omega,
the first and the last,
the beginning and the end."
✳ Revelation 22:13

No matter which route I've walked to Santiago I have always had mixed feelings in the last few days. Other pilgrims share this experience. It's a feeling of regret that the adventure and the freedom of the Camino is coming to an end. It's tinged with the excitement of going home, seeing loved ones again and wearing different clothes to the walking gear we've had on every day since we started the Camino. Some pilgrims actually slow down in the last few days to prolong their Camino just a little. But for all of us it comes to an end as we arrive in the Plaza Obradoiro, the great square in front of the magnificent Cathedral of Santiago. My bittersweet feelings about the Camino ending have always been erased by the excitement of arrival, the sense of achievement and celebration and the whoops of delight of the other pilgrims who pour into the square. Cyclists hold their cycles high like trophies. Walking pilgrims throw off their packs to embrace their companions. Some dance, some sing and some cry with happiness.

The square is majestic and is dominated by the mighty façade of the medieval cathedral, with many statues of Saint James gazing down on the jubilant pilgrims. It is as if that square encapsulates all of the life of Santiago. On one side stands the five-star Parador Hotel, said to be the oldest hotel in the world – because it started life to provide hospitality and medical care for sick and dying pilgrims in the Middle Ages. Facing the cathedral is the Palace of Rajoy, named after the archbishop who built it first to accommodate the priests of the cathedral who were needed in considerable numbers to hear the pilgrims' confessions. It is now the town hall, the political centre of Santiago city. The other building is the headquarters of the famous University of Santiago de Compostela which was founded in the Middle Ages. Church, state and pilgrim hospitality in one square, the place exudes history and tradition.

We pilgrims have our own traditions to follow after we arrive. Find a bed, visit the tomb of the apostle, hug the Saint, collect our Compostela in the Pilgrims' Office, attend the pilgrims' Mass.

There are many things to do in Santiago and you can get my book *A Pilgrim's Guide to Santiago de Compostela* which can tell you more about them, including walking the "Route of Routes", which touches on every Camino route as it enters the city. A great way to give any friends or relatives who have come to meet you a taste of the Camino.

Some pilgrims keep walking to Finisterre and Muxía, whilst others rest and explore Santiago until it is time for the journey home. No matter what we do, all of us reflect on the experience of the Camino, the challenges and the joys, the resolutions we have made to change our lives in some way. At home we'll tell people about the experience. Because it has been so good we might go on just a little too much. Perhaps when our loved ones get fed up listening to our Camino tales it is time to join the pilgrim association where you live so that you can meet like-minded Camino enthusiasts. Perhaps it will be time to plan your next Camino!

The very stones of the cathedral tell us our journey continues beyond the Camino, beyond Santiago. The doorway of the entrance to the cathedral, from the Plaza Platerias, is the oldest and is richly adorned with stone carvings. There is a *chrismom*, an emblem, with the symbols of the Greek letters Alpha and Omega carved

in relief. Unlike in the Greek alphabet, though, they are in reverse order so that Omega (the end) comes before Alpha (the beginning), symbolising that the end of our Camino is the beginning of the next part of our pilgrimage of life.

For me, my first arrival was very much a new beginning. After reaching the square I waited in a long line at the Pilgrims' Office, full of anticipation, and although my treatment at the desk was cursory, I was overjoyed to receive my Compostela. I went off to the cathedral for Mass and I was deeply moved that the pilgrims had made it their own: rucksacks were piled against the walls; pilgrims sat on the altar steps; the organ began and in the priests' procession I saw boots and bare legs beneath some of the vestments. The Botafumeiro (the great thurible) that flew over the pilgrims' heads was wonderful. At that Mass I realised deep in my heart that Santiago was where I wanted to be. I believe that this set off the chain of events which followed.

I knew I wanted to walk more and I decided on the Camino Inglés. The UK Pilgrim Association supplied some walking notes and asked if I would update them. As I started work on that first guidebook I also started a blog. I had only ever written management reports in the past and this was an incredibly refreshing development. I'm secretly quite shy and so I adopted the pen name Johnnie Walker. Well I'm Scottish and I like a dram! My idea was that there could be a series of inexpensive guidebooks written by pilgrims for pilgrims on a voluntary basis and anyone could be Johnnie Walker. However, the name stuck.

Soon more guidebook writing projects and Caminos followed and I eventually resigned from my full-time position. I started to spend more time in Santiago and became the first long-term volunteer at the Pilgrims' Office. One day, Danny, one of the staff who has become a close friend, explained that his family had an apartment which they didn't use. I went to see it. It had been the home of Danny's partner's grandmother who died. His partner's mother inherited it and, having totally refurbished it, sadly, she then died. Three bedrooms, two bathrooms, with views of the spires of the cathedral. It was like the *Marie Celeste*. I started using it on my visits, but I could not deny that the arrows were all pointing in one direction, and so I rented out my home in London and moved to Santiago to live for most of each year.

I love living in Santiago. There is plenty to do. In the pilgrim season I have lots of visitors and there are always pilgrims needing help and assistance. That might be visiting an English-speaking pilgrim in hospital, helping find a stolen rucksack, taking a pilgrim to the dentist or even welcoming four Irish pilgrims who rowed from Ireland! Each week brings something different. As for me, at this point in my journey along this holy road of Santiago, if anyone asks: "Did you meet God or come closer to God on your pilgrimage?" the answer is a resounding yes.

I'll be forever grateful that the Camino de Santiago helped me to understand that God is in the face of friends and the intimate companionship of walking the Way together. God is in the sign of peace which pilgrims of many nations share at Mass. God is in the pain, suffering and recovery of Helmut the drug addict and Zena the abused woman. God is in the breathtaking vistas, the flowers and animals, the path that never seems to end and God is in the kindness of strangers I have experienced on every Camino.

"How close are you to God now?" I ask myself. Not close enough… so it's about time I walked again!

"For the beauty of the earth,
For the beauty of the skies,
For the love which from our birth
Over and around us lies,
Lord of all, to thee we raise
This our grateful hymn of praise.

For the beauty of each hour
Of the day and of the night,
Hill and vale, and tree and flower,
Sun and moon and stars of light,
Lord of all, to thee we raise
This our grateful hymn of praise.

For the joy of human love,
Brother, sister, parent, child,
Friends on earth, and friends above,
Pleasures pure and undefiled,
Lord of all, to thee we raise
This our grateful hymn of praise."

✳ *Folliott S. Pierpoint* (1835-1917)

✳ My call to the Camino

Kay Caldwell

Mid-sixties. Recently widowed. A point in life when we either slip back into the life left over to live – which will never, ever be the same – or seek new challenges. A serendipitous meeting with an old friend revealed he had found new direction in walking the Camino de Santiago. "Try it", he said. No. I was definite. I wasn't fit enough, had bad feet. Much as I'd like to, it wasn't for me.

Serendipity visited again two weeks later when a group of friends invited me to join them on the Portuguese Camino. If I said "yes", it would happen. I said yes. I practised in an ever-increasing radius from my front door, building up the kilometres until I knew I could walk 26km in one day. Not comfortably, but I could do it. But I still doubted that I could do it day after day after day.

It turned out I could. A motley group of retired people – with an average age of seventy point two! – we set out from Tui (choosing what we thought the flattest route) and reached Santiago eight days later. I surprised myself. Each day's sore feet and aching limbs were always gone the next morning.

As we walked, we talked. Amongst us were Presbyterians and an atheist, and I was intrigued by their genuine appreciation of Catholic things that they saw and experienced along the way. The churches, the statues, the religious iconography, and Mass. I was seeing the Catholic Church I'd rejected through the eyes of others and it began to look different. Had I rejected it too easily? Spiritually, it seemed, I was going back to where I had started.

Since then, I've been embracing rather than turning from those aspects of the Church that I have difficulty with, pondering them rather than seeking alternatives. So, while the blisters heal, and strained calf muscles get better, it's tumbling to the truth about yourself that does irreparable good.

"Lead, kindly light, amid the encircling gloom,
lead thou me on.
The night is dark, and I am far from home;
lead thou me on.
O'er moor and fen, o'er crag and torrent,
till the night is gone.

I was not ever thus,
nor prayed that thou should lead me on.
I loved to choose and see my path,
but now: lead thou me on.
Keep thou my feet;
I do not ask to see the distant scene – one step enough for me.

Lead kindly light."

Adapted from the hymn by Saint John Henry Newman (1801-1890) ✳

Called to walk The Way

Filming *The Way* on the Camino to Santiago de Compostela was one of the most important and rewarding experiences of my life and it was, by far, the most satisfying role of my career.

It was filmed in 2009 over an eight-week schedule and followed the pilgrimage route from Saint Jean Pied de Port in the French Pyrenees across Northern Spain to Santiago, and on to Muxía for the final scene. The entire production was a family affair.

My son Emilio wrote and directed the film and played my character's son, Daniel, and our combined Camino experience inspired us to write the father/son memoir called *Along the Way*, which was published in 2012. My daughter, Renée, and my son Ramon each played small roles on screen and my wife, Janet, produced the film. When we needed completion funds, my son Charlie loaned us the final money. My father, Francisco Estevez, came from a tiny village in Galicia, Spain, not far from Santiago and *The Way* is dedicated to him "In Loving Memory".

But none of the above would have come to pass if not for my grandson, Taylor, and a beautiful young girl named Julia. These two met on the Camino at the casa rural called El Molino in Burgos in 2003. Gradually our two families grew together around the Camino, culminating with their wedding at El Molino in the summer of 2009 just before we began filming *The Way*.

Like the Camino itself *The Way* is truly a gift that keeps on giving. Since the film's release in 2011 it has inspired many thousands of people (mostly from the US and Canada) to make the pilgrimage, and many of those have shared their Camino experience with our family. But I must confess I have never actually made the full pilgrimage on foot myself,

"I think of the Camino as an opportunity to unite the will of the spirit with the work of the flesh."

✳ *Martin Sheen*

outside of my own performance in the film, and I still have a burning desire to do so. I think of the Camino as an opportunity to unite the will of the spirit with the work of the flesh. And though I know it's useless to regret the many lost opportunities I had to fulfil my dream, I continue to imagine myself out on the Camino in all seasons, at any number of familiar and sacred places and my spirit soars!

There I am leaving Saint Jean Pied de Port, walking to Roncesvalles, then on to Pamplona and before long I'm entering the gates at Burgos. Suddenly I'm arriving in León and I can see Cruz de Ferro in the distance, then before I know it I'm heading down the rainy slopes in Galicia to the steps of the Cathedral of Santiago! And all along the way, from every stranger and fellow pilgrim, from every open door and window of every house in every town and village, from every Mass in every church and every bunk in every shelter, from every patron in every bar, from every rock, every tree, every field and stream, from every wood and every hill and valley, from every bird and

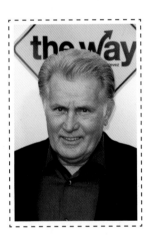

cloud in every sky, from every path and yellow shell that points the way, from *everywhere* and *everything* I hear the long promised blessing of "*Buen Camino.*"

Like a shouted "Hosanna" it is spontaneously and joyously bestowed! Yet I am reminded it is reserved solely for those on pilgrimage and I'm not among them… yet.

Perhaps next year or the following year, or sometime in the not-too-distant future all that may change. Meanwhile, *The Way* continues to fuel my imagination and inspire future pilgrims.

Buen Camino!
Martin Sheen

Thomas Avery in
The Way: Life is too big to walk it alone.

Where to get your Pilgrim Passport

and more information in your country

United Kingdom
www.facebook.com/groups/confraternitysaintjames/
www.csj.org.uk/prepare/get-your-credencial/

Ireland
www.facebook.com/Camino-Society-Ireland-110131172387472/
www.caminosociety.com/passport

United States of America
www.facebook.com/groups/AmericanPilgrims/
www.americanpilgrims.org/request-a-credential/

Canada
www.facebook.com/CanadianCompanyofPilgrims/
www.santiago.ca/memberships-credencials-and-badges/
www.duquebecacompostelle.org/

Australia
www.facebook.com/groups/AustralianPilgrimsontheCamino/
www.afotc.org/passport-credencial/

South Africa
www.facebook.com/groups/85195891935/
www.csjofsa.za.org/pilgrim-passport/

These forums are a great source of advice and information:
www.caminodesantiago.me/community/
www.caminodesantiago.org.uk/

About the author
Johnnie Walker

Scotsman John Rafferty is widely known in the Camino world as guide writer and author Johnnie Walker. John walked his first Camino to Santiago in 2007. That experience led to changes in his life he never expected. He gave up a career of thirty years as the Chief Executive of various national charities and senior positions in government and the National Health Service in the UK. He kept on walking more Camino routes and started to write guidebooks to the pilgrim routes in Spain and Portugal for the Confraternity of Saint James, the Pilgrims' Association in the UK. All of the proceeds of John's guidebooks go to this charity.

John eventually decided to live in Santiago de Compostela, where he started voluntary projects to help improve the welcome and care of English-speaking pilgrims. The Amigos Welcome Service was supported by all of the English-speaking pilgrim associations across the world and brought 300 volunteers to serve in Santiago for the first time. In the absence of any religious services in English in Santiago, John started the Camino Chaplaincy, bringing priests from the UK and Ireland to minister in Santiago and beyond. Both of these programmes were so successful that the Cathedral of Santiago now provides them as a permanent service for pilgrims. In 2012 John spearheaded the re-organisation, funding and re-opening of the church-run Albergue Fin del Camino in Santiago, which had closed. It remains open to this day as a viable facility for pilgrims in Santiago. In 2018 John proposed the development of a new Anglican Camino Chaplaincy which is now active in Santiago under the aegis of the Anglican Diocese in Europe. In 2019 the Camino Chaplaincy launched a new Camino Fund to encourage and support Young Leaders to take groups of young people on pilgrimage to Santiago. The proceeds of sales of this book will go towards that fund and pilgrim organisations.

In total John has published fifteen books, all of the profits of which go to support pilgrims in some way. In addition, he has raised over £200,000 for volunteering projects.

About the photographer
Miguel Castaño

Miguel Castaño was born in Madrid, where he began his career as a press photographer over forty years ago. Working with black-and-white images, he developed an interest in what he describes as "reporting and revealing". His images included many public figures such as politicians and actors, as well as ordinary people captured by his camera.

In 1982 Miguel gave up photography when he emigrated to Venezuela, where he lived for three years. That time living far away from his home country, family and friends was a period of life-changing discovery and spiritual experience which he describes as his "conversion". This inspired Miguel to have a different vision of how to use his talents as a photographer. Thus, when he returned to Spain in 1985 he moved from photographing in black and white to a more expressive range of images in light and colour. He left the press to focus on producing photographs which express life and faith.

Miguel and his wife, Inma, live in Santiago de Compostela with their two children, Laura and David, and two one-year-old identical twin grandsons.

Miguel's artwork is testimony to his faith. He shares it openly through his website: unabrisasuave.blogspot.com. "Una brisa suave" means "a gentle breeze". Miguel paraphrases a passage from the Book of Kings which he says encapsulates the profound change in his life:

The Lord was not in the storm. After the storm came the earthquake but the Lord was not in the earthquake. After the earthquake there was fire but the Lord was not in the fire. After the fire blew a gentle breeze.

For Miguel, welcoming the "gentle breeze" of the Lord to blow in his heart changed everything and inspired his photographs which he has donated to this book.